Insect World

Wasps

by Mari Schuh

Bullfrog
Books

Ideas for Parents and Teachers

Bullfrog Books let children practice reading informational text at the earliest reading levels. Repetition, familiar words, and photo labels support early readers.

Before Reading

• Discuss the cover photo. What does it tell them?

• Look at the picture glossary together. Read and discuss the words.

Read the Book

• "Walk" through the book and look at the photos. Let the child ask questions. Point out the photo labels.

• Read the book to the child, or have him or her read independently.

After Reading

• Prompt the child to think more. Ask: Have you ever seen a wasp? What kind of nest did it have?

Bullfrog Books are published by Jump!
5357 Penn Avenue South
Minneapolis, MN 55419
www.jumplibrary.com

Library of Congress Cataloging-in-Publication Data

Schuh, Mari C., 1975- author.
  Wasps / by Mari Schuh.
    pages cm. -- (Insect world)
  Summary: "This photo-illustrated book for early readers tells about the different nests built by wasps. Includes picture glossary"-- Provided by publisher.
  Audience: Ages 5 to 8.
  Audience: K to grade 3.
  Includes bibliographical references and index.
  ISBN 978-1-62031-088-5 (hardcover) --
ISBN 978-1-62496-156-4 (ebook)
  1. Wasps--Juvenile literature. I. Title.
II. Series: Schuh, Mari C., 1975- Insect world.
  SB945.W3
  595.79--dc23
                                    2013039898

Series Editor: Rebecca Glaser
Series Designer: Ellen Huber
Book Designer: Anna Peterson
Photo Researcher: Kurtis Kinneman

All photos by Shutterstock except: iStock, 21; Natasha Mhatre, 6, 6–7, 23tr; Nature Picture Library, 20–21; Superstock/Animals Animals, 10–11, 14-15, 16-17, 23br

Printed in the United States of America at Corporate Graphics, in North Mankato, Minnesota.
6-2014
10 9 8 7 6 5 4 3 2 1

Dedicated to Mona and Dan Schuh—MS

Table of Contents

Nest Makers

Buzz! Buzz!

Wasps are hard at work.

They are making nests.

Look!

It's a potter wasp.

She makes her nest alone.

She uses mud.

nest

Paper wasps make a nest.
They chew wood.

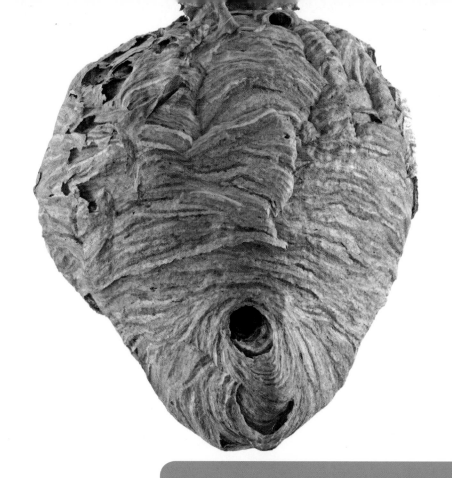

They add spit.
They make a paste.
It dries into paper.

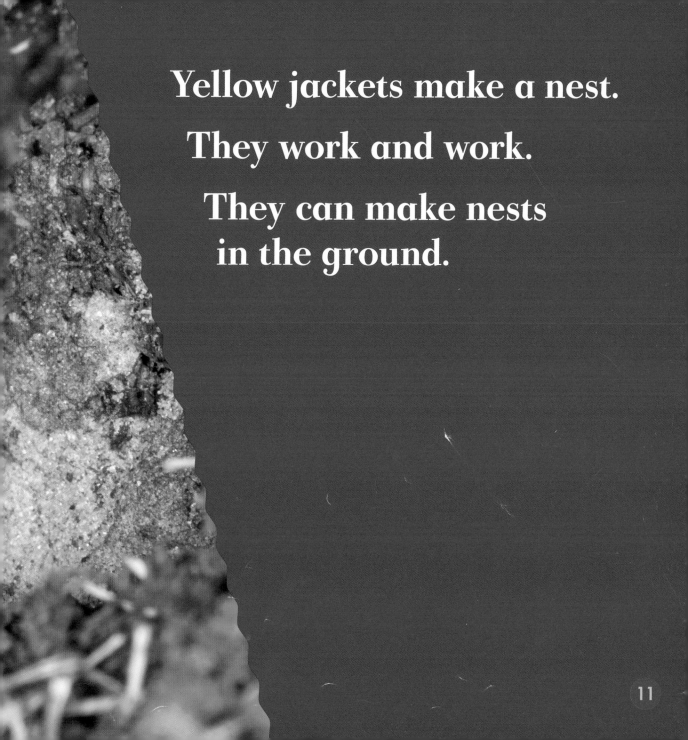

Yellow jackets make a nest.
They work and work.
They can make nests
in the ground.

cell

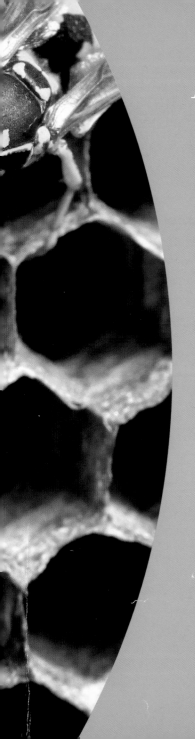

A nest holds eggs.
See the cells?
Each cell holds one egg.

Look!

A wasp catches a bug.

It puts the bug
in the nest.

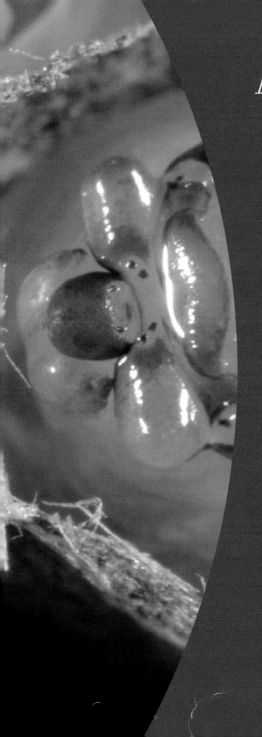

An egg hatches.

A young wasp grows.

It eats the bug.

Wasps keep the nest safe.

See their bright colors?

The colors keep enemies away.

Go away!

Ouch!

Females sting enemies.
Now the nest is safe.

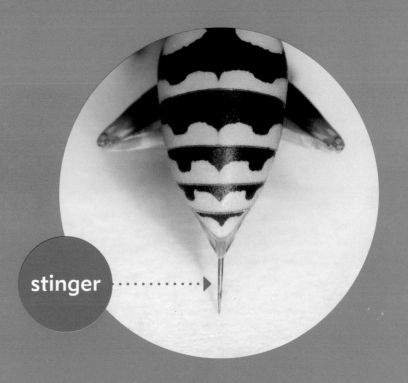

stinger ·········▶

Parts of a Wasp

wings
A wasp has four thin wings.

antenna
A wasp uses these to smell and feel.

waist
A wasp has a narrow waist.

jaws
A wasp has strong jaws.

leg
A wasp has six legs, like all insects.

Picture Glossary

cell
A tiny room inside a nest; cells have six sides.

potter wasp
A kind of wasp that lives alone. Potter wasps make nests that look like tiny pots.

paper wasp
A kind of wasp that lives in a group and makes paper-like nests.

yellow jacket
A kind of wasp that lives in groups and may build nests under the ground.

Index

To Learn More

Learning more is as easy as 1, 2, 3.

1) Go to www.factsurfer.com

2) Enter "wasps" into the search box.

3) Click the "Surf" button to see a list of websites.

With factsurfer.com, finding more information is just a click away.